RED PANDA

BY TYLER GRADY

Dylanna Press

Copyright © 2024 by Dylanna Press
Author: Tyler Grady

All rights reserved. No part of this publication may be reproduced, stored in a retrieval system, or transmitted by any means, including electronic, mechanical, photocopying, or otherwise, without prior written permission of the publisher.

Although the publisher has taken all reasonable care in the preparation of this book, we make no warranty about the accuracy or completeness of its content and, to the maximum extent permitted, disclaim all liability arising from its use.

Trademarks: Dylanna Press is a registered trademark of Dylanna Publishing, Inc. and may not be used without written permission.

ISBN: 978-1647904128
Publisher: Dylanna Publishing, Inc.
First Edition: 2024
10 9 8 7 6 5 4 3 2 1

For information about special discounts for bulk purchases, please contact:

Dylanna Publishing, Inc.
www.dylannapublishing.com

Contents

Meet the Red Panda　　　　7

What Do Red Pandas Look Like?　　　8

Where Do Red Pandas Live?　　　11

Physical Adaptations　　　12

What Do Red Pandas Eat?　　　15

Social Life　　　16

Territory　　　19

Day in the Life　　　20

Mating and Birth　　　23

Growing Up Red Panda　　　24

Red Pandas and Their Ecosystem　　　27

Lifespan and Predators　　　28

Threats and Challenges　　　31

Seasonal Molting　　　32

Conclusion　　　35

Test Your Red Panda Knowledge!　　　36

STEM Challenge: Think Like a Scientist!　　　37

Word Search　　　38

Glossary　　　39

Resources and References　　　40

Index　　　41

Meet the Red Panda

Red pandas are mammals that are native to the eastern Himalayas and southwestern China. They can be found in the countries of Nepal, India, Bhutan, Myanmar, and China.

Despite having "panda" in their name, red pandas are not related to giant pandas but are rather the only species in their own unique family, Ailuridae. They are sometimes called "firefoxes" due to their reddish-brown fur and bushy tails.

Their scientific name is *Ailurus fulgens*, which means "fire-colored cat," reflecting their vibrant fur and cat-like appearance. Their closest relatives are raccoons, skunks, and weasels.

DID YOU KNOW?

Red pandas aren't actually pandas! They belong to their own unique family, separate from both bears and giant pandas.

What Do Red Pandas Look Like?

Red pandas have a unique and striking appearance. They are about the size of a domestic cat, with a body length of 20 to 25 inches (50 to 64 cm) and a tail that adds another 12 to 20 inches (30 to 50 cm). They typically weigh between 7 to 14 pounds (3 to 6 kg).

Red pandas have round heads with large, pointed ears and a short snout. Their face is mostly white with reddish-brown "tear" marks extending from their eyes to the corner of their mouth. They have a soft, dense coat that is reddish-brown in color, with black fur on their legs and belly. This reddish-brown and black coloration helps them blend in with the mossy branches and foliage of their habitat.

DID YOU KNOW?

A red panda's thick fur isn't just red — even the bottoms of their feet are covered in fur to help them walk on snow without slipping!

One of the most distinctive features of red pandas is their long, bushy tail. The tail has alternating red and buff rings and measures almost as long as their body. They use their tail for balance and to wrap around themselves for warmth in cold temperatures.

Where Do Red Pandas Live?

Red pandas are arboreal animals, which means they spend most of their time in trees. They inhabit the temperate forests of the eastern Himalayas and southwestern China, at elevations between 5,000 and 15,000 feet (1,500 to 4,500 meters).

Their habitat is characterized by steep, mountainous terrain with dense forests of coniferous trees, deciduous hardwoods, and bamboo thickets. The trees provide red pandas with shelter, food, and a place to rest and sleep during the day.

Red pandas are adapted to cooler climates due to the high elevations of their habitat. They have a thick, woolly undercoat covered by long, coarse guard hairs that protect them from cold temperatures and wet conditions. However, they are not well-suited to extremely cold weather and may descend to lower elevations during the winter months.

Red pandas are well-adapted to life in the trees. They are agile climbers, using their sharp, semi-retractable claws and false "thumb" to navigate through the branches with ease. Their ankles are extremely flexible, capable of rotating 180 degrees, which allows them to climb headfirst down tree trunks. Additionally, their long, bushy tail helps them maintain balance as they move through the treetops.

Physical Adaptations

The red panda has several physical adaptations that help them thrive in their forest habitat.

- **False Thumb:** Red pandas have a unique adaptation called a "false thumb," which is an enlarged wrist bone that functions like an opposable thumb. This allows them to grip bamboo stems and tree branches more easily.

- **Sharp Claws:** Their sharp, semi-retractable claws provide excellent traction for climbing trees and navigating through their mountainous habitat.

- **Flexible Ankles:** Red panda ankles can rotate 180 degrees, enabling them to climb down trees headfirst. This flexibility also helps them navigate through the tree canopy with ease.

- **Thick Fur:** Their dense, woolly undercoat and long, coarse guard hairs protect them from cold temperatures and wet conditions in their high-elevation habitat.

- **Camouflage:** The reddish-brown and black coloration of their fur helps them blend in with the mossy branches and reddish-brown foliage of their surroundings.

- **Specialized Teeth:** Like other members of the order Carnivora, red pandas have specialized teeth for eating meat, but they have adapted to a primarily herbivorous diet. Their sharp incisors and canines are used for biting and tearing bamboo, while their flattened molars are used for crushing and grinding fibrous plant material.

- **Digestive System:** Red pandas have an enlarged digestive tract that allows them to process their high-fiber, low-nutrient diet of bamboo efficiently.

- **Bushy Tail:** Their long, bushy tail aids in balance as they navigate through the trees and can be wrapped around their body for warmth and protection from the elements.

These adaptations help red pandas to be well-suited for life in their unique forest habitat.

What Do Red Pandas Eat?

Red pandas are primarily plant eaters, with bamboo constituting the majority of their diet. In fact, bamboo makes up about 95 percent of their diet in the wild.

Despite their specialization for eating bamboo, red pandas are also known to eat other foods such as fruits, berries, mushrooms, roots, acorns, lichens, bird eggs, and occasionally small mammals and birds. This varies depending on the season and the availability of different food sources in their habitat.

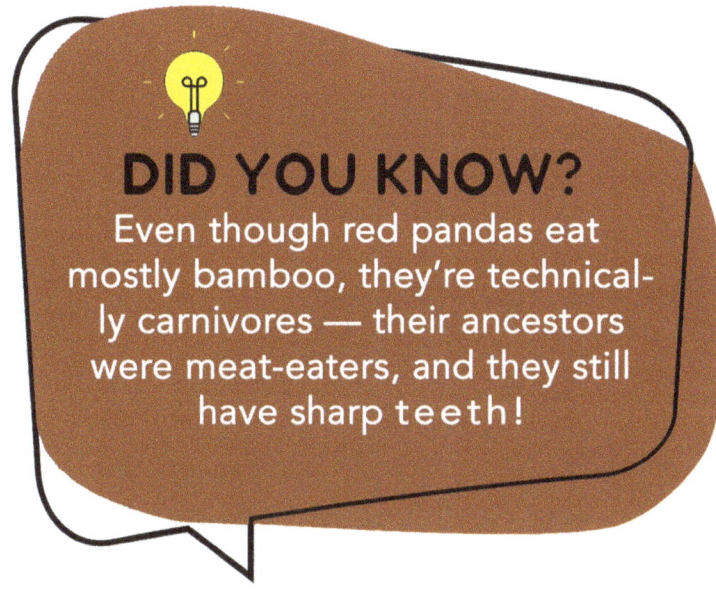

DID YOU KNOW?
Even though red pandas eat mostly bamboo, they're technically carnivores — their ancestors were meat-eaters, and they still have sharp teeth!

Red pandas are most active during early morning and late afternoon, spending much of their time foraging for food. Despite their small size, they have a low metabolic rate, which means they need to spend a significant portion of their day eating to meet their energy requirements.

Unlike true herbivores, red pandas have a simple stomach but a very long intestine that helps them digest their fibrous diet, primarily composed of bamboo. This long digestive tract is crucial for extracting maximum nutrients from their relatively nutrient-poor diet.

Water is an essential part of their diet, and red pandas get most of the water they need from the bamboo they eat. However, they will also drink fresh water when it is available.

Social Life

Red pandas are generally solitary animals, typically found alone or in small family groups consisting of a mother and her cubs.

During the breeding season, red pandas interact more frequently. Males and females will communicate through various vocalizations, including whistles, snorts, and squeals. These vocalizations are used to establish territories, attract mates, and communicate with their young.

DID YOU KNOW?

Red pandas communicate by whistling, squeaking, and using scent marks — they even rub special glands on trees to leave messages for others.

Although they are generally solitary, red pandas exhibit some social behaviors. They have been observed playing with one another, especially young cubs.

Red pandas have a solitary social structure that is adapted to their arboreal lifestyle. While they do not live in large social groups, they still exhibit important social behaviors and interactions, particularly during the breeding season and when raising their young.

Territory

Red pandas are territorial animals, with males and females establishing and defending their own territories. The size of their territories varies depending on the availability of food and other resources but generally ranges from 1 to 8 square kilometers (0.4 to 3 square miles). Males tend to have larger territories than females.

Red pandas mark their territories using scent glands located on their feet and at the base of their tail. They leave a musky scent on trees, rocks, and other objects within their territory, communicating their presence to other red pandas and helping to avoid territorial disputes.

These animals are generally non-migratory and remain within their established territories. However, they may make seasonal movements to different parts of their range in response to changes in food availability or weather conditions.

Red pandas do not build specific structures for shelter. Instead, they rely on naturally occurring sites such as hollow trees, stumps, rock crevices, or dense thickets of bamboo. These sites provide protection from predators and the elements, as well as a place to rest and sleep.

Day in the Life

Red pandas live life on their own cozy schedule. They're crepuscular, meaning they're most active during the cool, quiet hours of dawn and dusk. When the sun climbs high, they retreat into the treetops to nap among the branches, where the shade keeps them cool and hidden from predators.

During the day, these fluffy climbers curl up high above the forest floor, wrapping their bushy tails around their faces like blankets to stay warm. Sometimes they nap for up to 16 hours a day—but don't be fooled! Even in sleep, red pandas stay alert, their sharp hearing ready to catch the faintest rustle of danger below.

DID YOU KNOW?

Each red panda has its own distinct facial markings, like a fingerprint, helping researchers tell individuals apart in the wild.

When they're awake, red pandas are almost always eating. Their favorite food, bamboo, doesn't offer much nutrition, so they must munch through large amounts every day—chewing, stripping, and crunching their way through tender shoots and leaves.

Between meals, they take time to groom their thick fur, rub scent glands on branches to mark territory, and occasionally cross paths with other red pandas. Most of the year, they prefer solitude—but during the breeding season, the forest becomes livelier with chirps, whistles, and soft squeaks.

Living in the misty, temperate forests of the Himalayas, red pandas have mastered the art of balance—resting when it's hot, moving when it's cool, and blending into the rhythm of the forest itself.

Mating and Birth

Red pandas are polygynandrous, which means that both males and females may mate with multiple partners during the breeding season. This mating system increases genetic diversity within the population.

The breeding season for red pandas typically occurs from late fall to early winter, with most mating occurring between mid-January and early February. During this period, males exhibit increased activity including vocalizations and extensive scent marking to attract females and assert dominance over competitors.

After a gestation period of about 4.5 months, the female red panda will give birth to a litter of 1 to 4 cubs, typically in a den located in a hollow tree or rock crevice.

Red panda cubs are born blind and helpless, weighing only about 3 to 4 ounces (85 to 113 grams) at birth.

Growing Up Red Panda

Cubs are altricial, meaning they are born in an undeveloped state and depend entirely on their mother for care. The mother will nurse and care for her cubs for several months, keeping them hidden in the den for the first few weeks of life.

As the cubs grow and develop, the mother will gradually introduce them to solid food, typically starting with tender bamboo shoots. She will also teach them essential skills such as climbing, foraging, and avoiding predators.

Red panda fathers do not participate in raising the cubs, as they are solitary animals outside of the breeding season. The mother is solely responsible for the care and protection of her young.

Cubs will stay with their mother until they are about a year old. After this period, they start to seek independence, venturing out to establish their own territories and beginning the cycle anew.

> **DID YOU KNOW?**
> These amazing climbers can rotate their ankles to climb down trees headfirst — something even squirrels struggle to do!

Red Pandas and Their Ecosystem

Red pandas play a unique and important role within their ecosystems.

As red pandas forage for bamboo they help to maintain the balance of vegetation in their habitat. By selectively feeding on bamboo leaves and shoots, they prevent the plants from overtaking other vegetation, allowing a diversity of plant species to thrive in the forest understory.

Red pandas also contribute to seed dispersal. As they eat various fruits and berries, the seeds pass through their digestive system and are eventually deposited throughout the forest via their droppings. This process helps to propagate different plant species and maintain the biodiversity of the ecosystem.

DID YOU KNOW?
Red pandas use their tails like blankets, wrapping them around their bodies to stay warm in freezing mountain weather.

The droppings also provide a valuable food source for a variety of insects and enrich the soil with essential nutrients. This, in turn, supports the growth and overall health of the forest.

One unique ecological interaction involves a species of moss found in the shaded branches of fir trees, which are favored resting spots for red pandas. This moss benefits from the nitrogen-rich droppings of red pandas, which in turn provides a comfortable and camouflaged resting place for them. This is an example of a mutually beneficial relationship.

Red pandas also serve as prey for larger predators, such as snow leopards and martens. By being a part of the food chain, they contribute to the survival of these predators and help maintain the natural order within their habitat.

Lifespan and Predators

The average lifespan of a red panda is 8 to 10 years in the wild. In captivity, where they are free from predators and receive regular veterinary care, red pandas can live longer, often up to 15 years, there have even been instances where they lived to be over 20 years.

In their natural habitat, red pandas are prey to several large carnivores. Their primary predators include snow leopards, and martens. Birds of prey such as eagles and hawks also pose a threat, particularly to younger or smaller red pandas.

DID YOU KNOW?
Fewer than 10,000 red pandas remain in the wild. Protecting their bamboo forests in the Himalayas is the only way to keep this species from disappearing.

Additionally, smaller mammals like foxes and wild dogs can be predators, especially targeting juvenile red pandas or those that are sick and weaker.

To protect themselves from these threats, red pandas utilize their exceptional climbing skills and the camouflage provided by their fur. When threatened, they can quickly escape into the treetops, using their sharp claws and agility to navigate through the branches. Their reddish-brown fur helps them blend in with the mossy branches and foliage of their habitat, making it harder for predators to spot them.

Threats and Challenges

Aside from predators, red pandas face other threats and challenges, many of them human related:

- **Habitat Loss and Fragmentation**: Deforestation, land conversion for agriculture, and human settlement have led to the loss and fragmentation of red panda habitat. As their natural home is destroyed or divided, red pandas find it increasingly difficult to find food, mates, and suitable den sites.

- **Poaching and Illegal Trade:** Despite being protected by law, red pandas are still poached for their distinctive fur, which is used to make hats, clothing, and other decorative items. They are also captured and sold illegally as exotic pets.

- **Climate Change:** As global temperatures rise, the mountain forests that red pandas inhabit are changing. Alterations in the timing and intensity of seasons can affect the availability of bamboo, their primary food source, and disrupt their breeding cycles.

- **Human-Wildlife Conflict:** As human populations expand into red panda territory, there is an increased risk of conflict. Red pandas may enter agricultural areas in search of food, leading to potential retaliation from farmers.

- **Disease:** Red pandas are susceptible to various diseases, some of which can be transmitted by domestic animals like dogs. Canine distemper virus, for example, has been known to cause mortality in red panda populations.

Conservation efforts are crucial to lessen these threats and ensure the survival of red pandas in the wild. Initiatives such as habitat protection, anti-poaching patrols, community education, and captive breeding programs are being implemented to safeguard the future of this unique and fascinating species.

Seasonal Molting

When seasons change, red pandas go through a fascinating process called molting. This is when they shed their old fur to make way for new, healthy fur to grow in its place.

Red pandas molt twice a year—once in the spring and once in the fall. In the spring, they lose their heavy winter coat so they can stay cool in the warmer months. In the fall, they grow a thicker, warmer coat to get ready for the cold winter.

During molting, red pandas might look a little funny as they lose patches of old fur. This happens gradually, starting at their head and moving down to their tail. It can take a few weeks for all the old fur to fall out. Red pandas will groom themselves more during this time to help get rid of the loose fur.

As the old fur comes out, new fur grows in. This new coat tends to be brighter and healthier, aiding in camouflage against the mossy branches and fallen leaves of their habitat. The new fur is crucial not only for blending in but also for maintaining optimal body temperature in varying climates.

Molting takes a lot of energy, so red pandas need to eat more during this time to help their new fur grow in strong and healthy. Their bamboo diet is especially important for getting the right nutrients.

In addition to helping red pandas adjust to the changing seasons, molting also helps keep their skin and fur healthy by removing any parasites or irritations that might have built up over time.

So, while red pandas may look a bit patchy during their molting process, it's all part of their amazing adaptation to life in the forest. When it's done, they'll have a fresh, beautiful coat that keeps them cozy and camouflaged in their forest home.

Conclusion

Red pandas are truly fascinating and enchanting creatures that capture our hearts with their striking appearance, adorable behavior, and unique adaptations. However, despite their popularity and charm, red pandas are facing significant threats in the wild, and their future is uncertain.

The International Union for Conservation of Nature (IUCN) classifies red pandas as an endangered species, indicating that they are at a high risk of extinction in the near future. Recent estimates suggest that there are fewer than 10,000 mature red pandas left in the wild, with some studies indicating the number could be as low as 2,500. This fragmented population is scattered across their range in the eastern Himalayas and southwestern China, making them even more vulnerable.

Conservation efforts are underway to safeguard the future of red pandas. Organizations like the Red Panda Network, World Wildlife Fund (WWF), zoos, and wildlife sanctuaries are working to protect habitats, combat poaching, educate communities, and maintain genetic diversity through captive breeding programs.

By supporting these conservation initiatives, spreading awareness, and promoting sustainable practices, we can contribute to a brighter future for red pandas. Through understanding, compassion, and dedicated action, we can help ensure that these unique and wonderful animals continue to thrive in their natural habitats, playing their vital role in the delicate balance of the mountain forest ecosystems they call home.

Test Your Red Panda Knowledge!

Think you know these adorable forest climbers? Test your knowledge about the red panda—the fluffy, tree-loving acrobat of the Himalayas!

1. What is the red panda's scientific name?
A) Ailurus fulgens   B) Panda minor   C) Ursus rufus   D) Procyon panda

2. True or False: Red pandas are closely related to giant pandas.

3. Where do red pandas live in the wild?
A) Deserts of Africa   B) Mountains of Asia   C) Forests of South America
D) Grasslands of Australia

4. What do red pandas eat most of the time?
A) Meat and fish   B) Bamboo leaves and shoots   C) Fruits and honey   D) Insects and eggs

5. What special adaptation helps red pandas grip branches?
A) Webbed feet   B) Sharp claws and flexible ankles   C) Long tails for balance only   D) Sticky pads

6. What is a red panda's tail used for?
A) Storing food   B) Balance and warmth   C) Communication   D) Scaring predators

7. When are red pandas most active?
A) During the day   B) At night and early morning   C) In winter only   D) After rainfall

8. What is a baby red panda called?
A) Kit   B) Pup   C) Cub   D) Joey

9. What is the biggest threat to red pandas in the wild?
A) Polar bears   B) Habitat loss and deforestation   C) Freezing weather   D) Competition with monkeys

10. What is the red panda's conservation status?
A) Least Concern   B) Vulnerable   C) Endangered   D) Extinct in the Wild

Answer Key: 1. A   2. False   3. B   4. B   5. B   6. B   7. B   8. A   9. B   10. C

STEM Challenge: Think Like a Scientist!

Red pandas are incredible climbers that spend much of their lives in the trees. Their long tails and thick fur help them survive the cold mountain forests of Asia. Try these experiments to discover how these unique adaptations work!

Balancing Tail Test

Topic: Balance and Motion

You'll Need:
Ruler or long stick, small weights (coins or erasers), tape, a friend

What to Do:
1. Tape one or two coins to one end of the ruler.
2. Hold the ruler horizontally with one hand and try to balance it.
3. Now add a coin or two to the other end and see how it changes.
4. Try walking slowly while keeping it balanced—does it help?

What You'll Learn:
A red panda's long, bushy tail helps it balance as it walks along narrow branches. The tail also acts like a warm blanket when they curl up to sleep in cold weather!

Stay-Warm Fur Test

Topic: Insulation and Adaptation

You'll Need:
Two small bowls, warm water, ice cubes, plastic wrap, towel

What to Do:
1. Fill both bowls halfway with warm water.
2. Cover one bowl with plastic wrap and wrap a towel around it.
3. Leave the other bowl uncovered.
4. Add a few ice cubes to each and wait 10 minutes.
5. Which bowl stayed warmer?

What You'll Learn:
Red pandas live in cold Himalayan forests and stay warm thanks to their thick double-layered fur. The towel acts like fur insulation, trapping body heat just like a red panda's coat does in freezing mountain air!

Word Search

```
R O C G U X Y Y R A T I L O S U A T
Y O E J U V G C R R G P F J B Q W K
H E I J F M A M M A L S Q O N M C F
I D O R A B U K B N D K R A K X A C
N O I T A Z I L A C O V U Q H L M R
D E K R E A D I R U L I A G A B O E
Q B I O D I V E R S I T Y I A E U P
J J N A P S E K X B S N R L M T F U
V V H T D L O I I F N O P E D A L S
A F E M I A L U I L T I T J U R A C
F G O G N U P F X I G S U L B C G U
T O A R V C T T R H Y X A P M I E L
S A O M A D G R A S E E E A U L O A
P F I D I G E Z O T R O R G H O J R
O I X L C T E C K O I M L N T B B Q
T R T S R H E R B C P O V A E A A M
E E I G F V A R O M F C N P S T M Z
E F O J K Z A I P P W L S S L E B I
R O O C C H J L N J F O V R A M O W
T X C N R H E R B I V O R E F U O O
```

Adaptations	Crepuscular	Mammals
Agile	Ecosystem	Metabolic Rate
Ailuridae	False Thumb	Solitary
Arboreal	Firefox	Tail
Bamboo	Food Chain	Territorial
Biodiversity	Forage	Treetops
Camouflage	Herbivore	Vocalization

Glossary

adaptations – special body features or behaviors that help an animal survive in its environment

bamboo – a fast-growing plant that looks like grass but grows tall and woody; red pandas eat its leaves and shoots

camouflage – coloring or markings that help an animal blend into its surroundings to stay safe from predators

carnivore – an animal that eats meat; red pandas are in the order Carnivora but mostly eat plants

claws – sharp, curved nails used for climbing trees and grasping food

conservation – protecting wildlife, forests, and natural habitats for future generations

ecosystem – a community of living things and their environment working together as one system

endangered – at serious risk of extinction in the wild

habitat – the natural home or environment where an animal lives

herbivore – an animal that eats mostly plants, such as bamboo, berries, and leaves

nocturnal – active mainly at night and sleeping during the day

omnivore – an animal that eats both plants and small animals

predator – an animal that hunts and eats other animals for food

solitary – living alone most of the time instead of in large groups

tail – the long, bushy part of an animal's body that helps with balance and warmth

Resources and References

Want to learn more about red pandas and mountain forest wildlife? Check out these trusted books, websites, and organizations dedicated to understanding and protecting these charming, tree-dwelling mammals.

Books

Red Pandas: A Complete Guide by Angela R. Glatston (Academic Press) — Comprehensive research on red panda biology, behavior, and conservation.

National Geographic Kids Readers: Red Pandas by Laura Marsh — Fun facts, vivid photos, and accessible science for young readers.

The Smallest Bear: The Story of the Red Panda by Nicola Davies (Walker Books) — A beautifully illustrated look at red pandas and the importance of protecting their forests.

Wildlife of the Himalayas by Bikram Grewal (Princeton University Press) — An overview of animals and ecosystems in the Himalayan mountain range, home to red pandas.

Websites

National Geographic Kids – Red Panda Facts
kids.nationalgeographic.com/animals/mammals/facts/red-panda
Fun and educational facts, photos, and videos about red pandas.

Red Panda Network
www.redpandanetwork.org
An organization dedicated exclusively to protecting red pandas and their forest habitats through community-based conservation.

World Wildlife Fund (WWF) – Red Panda
www.worldwildlife.org/species/red-panda
Learn about threats to red pandas, their forest ecosystems, and global efforts to save them.

Wildlife Conservation Society (WCS) – Asia Programs
www.wcs.org
Information on wildlife protection across Asia, including red panda habitat regions.

Keep Exploring!

If you enjoyed learning about lions, explore other titles in the *This Incredible Planet* series to discover more amazing animals—from sea turtles to penguins to elephants—and the habitats they call home.

INDEX

adaptations, 9, 10
Ailurus fulgens, 5
ankles, 9, 10
appearance, 6
arboreal animals, 9, 14
bamboo, 13, 18, 25
biodiversity, 25
breeding, 14, 21
camouflage, 10, 26, 30
claws, 9, 10, 26
climate change, 29
conservation, 29, 33
crespuscular animals, 18
cubs, 21, 22
diet, 13, 18
digestive system, 10, 13
disease, 29
ecosystems, 25
endangered species, 33
false thumb, 9, 10
food chain, 25
foraging, 13, 18, 25
fur, 6, 10, 26, 30
genetic diversity, 21
habitat, 5, 9, 33
habitat loss, 29

herbivores, 13
humans, 29
lifespan, 26
mammals, 5
mating, 21
metabolic rate, 13
molting, 30
moss, 25
parenting, 22
physical characteristics, 6
poaching, 29
population, 33
predators, 25, 26
relatives, 5
reproduction, 21
seed dispersal, 25
senses, 18
size, 6
sleep, 18
social behaviors, 14
tail, 6, 9, 10, 18
teeth, 10
territories, 17
threats, 26, 29, 33
vocalizations, 14
water, 13

www.ingramcontent.com/pod-product-compliance
Lightning Source LLC
Chambersburg PA
CBHW040224040426
42333CB00051B/3437